The

of Ruth

Words, Thoughts & Inspiration

from Ruth Bader Ginsburg

compiled by

Kathryn & Ross Petras

ISBN 978-0-9904693-3-9

cover: modified "illustration of Ruth Bader Ginsburg" by Coreypkolb used under Creative Commons Attribution-Share Alike 4.0 International license
https://commons.wikimedia.org/wiki/File:Ruth_Bader_Ginsburg_Illustration.jpg

published by Off the Wall Books

Printed in the United States of America
First printing September 2020

Foreword

It's no surprise that when she was well over 80, Ruth Bader Ginsburg became known by the rapper moniker "The Notorious R.B.G." A rapper name for a distinguished Supreme Court Justice? Well, why not?

R.B.G was often so far ahead of her times that only a name like that would really fit. She broke down barriers, fought for the underrepresented, the discriminated against, and the overlooked. She was a champion of feminism and equality long before the 1960s feminist revolution.

She almost had to be — she was only one of nine women in her entering class at Harvard Law School, with no female law professors, and she faced sex discrimination head on. She went on to tackle sex discrimination cases referred to her by the ACLU and, under her leadership, ACLU Women's Rights Project was born.

She didn't stop there. When she was appointed to the Supreme Court Bench in 1993 she went on fighting, not only for women and minorities, but for all of us. She saw the USA as a work in progress and said that giving the dispossessed their rights wouldn't mean taking away rights from others but would mean more rights for all.

In short, she was a legal icon, a visionary, a fighter, and, in the words of Harvard Law School professor Daphna Renan, "tenacious, unflappable and deeply wise."

She also had a wicked sense of humor. Not surprisingly she absolutely loved being called The Notorious R.B.G.

She early on realized that to create change, you've got to not only get along with people very different from you. Her "best buddy" on the Supreme Court was conversative justice Antonin Scalia. A staunch proponent of women's reproductive rights friends with a staunch opponent of those rights? Well, again, why not?

That never meant that she didn't fight him vociferously on the bench. As she once said of her conservative friend: "I love him. But sometimes I'd like to strangle him." (Typical of her careful legal mind, she actually changed the wording of what she initially said about her right wing friend. She first said she wanted to "wring his neck." But upon reflection, she thought that sounded a little too aggressive — and after all, her mother always told her to act like a lady!) And so while she vigorously fought Scalia in court, she also considered him one of her best friends, particularly because they both really enjoyed a good joke. In fact she said she sometimes had trouble keeping from laughing as he whispered jokes to her during solemn but sometimes very dull court proceedings. That's a wonderful picture of a great Justice.

This unusual friendship shows Ruth Bader Ginsburg at her best: uncompromising in her beliefs but always willing to listen to and even laugh with the other side. This is why her death, in these fractured, divided times, is all the more tragic. Especially now, we need more people like her.

And so we've compiled this book: a collection of our favorite quotations and thoughts from Ruth Bader Ginsburg. We've gathered not only the more usual shorter quotes but also some longer passages that really give us insight into her nuanced life and her ideas. Ruth Bader Ginsburg may no longer be with us but her words, her ideas and her example will surely endure.

Fight for the things that you care about. But do it in a way that will lead others to join you.

It was beyond my wildest imagination that I would one day become The Notorious R.B.G.

I think unconscious bias is one of the hardest things to get at. My favorite example is the symphony orchestra. When I was growing up, there were no women in orchestras. Auditioners thought they could tell the difference between a woman playing and a man. Some intelligent person devised a simple solution: Drop a curtain between the auditioners and the people trying out. And, lo and behold, women began to get jobs in symphony orchestras. When I told this story a couple of years ago, there was a violinist who said, "But you left out one thing. Not only do we audition behind a curtain, but we audition shoeless, so they won't hear a woman's heels coming onstage."

So often in life,
things that you
regard as an
impediment turn
out to be great,
good fortune.

I do think that I was born under a very bright star … I went to law school when women were less than 3% of lawyers in the country; today, they are 50%. I

never had a
woman teacher in
college or in law
school. The
changes have
been enormous.
And … they've
gone much too
far [to be] going
back.

Real change,
enduring
change,
happens one
step at a time.

We have the oldest
written constitution
still in force in the
world, and it starts
out with three
words,
"We, the people."

Anybody who has
been discriminated
against, who comes
from a group that's
been discriminated
against, knows
what it's like.

One of my greatest pleasures as a child was sitting on my mother's lap when she would read to me, and then going to the library with her. In fact, she deposited me in the children's section of the library and went to get her hair done. By the time she'd come back, I had the five books that I would take home for that week.

It is not
women's
liberation, it is
women's and
men's
liberation.

At Cornell University, my professor of European literature, Vladimir Nabokov, changed the way I read and the way I write. Words could paint pictures, I learned from him. Choosing the right word, and the right word order, he illustrated, could make an enormous difference in conveying an image or an idea.

Women belong in all places where decisions are being made.

America is known as a country that welcomes people to its shores. All kinds of people. The image of the Statue of Liberty with Emma Lazarus' famous poem. She lifts her lamp and welcomes people to the golden shore, where they

will not experience
prejudice because of
the color of their
skin, the religious
faith that they follow.

We are at last beginning to relegate to the history books the idea of the token woman.

I read every federal case that had to do with women's equality or the lack thereof and every law review article. Now that seems like it was quite an undertaking but, in fact, it was easily manageable because there was so little.

The written argument endures. The oral argument is fleeting.

I read Simone de Beauvoir's *Second Sex* and that was an eye-opener. So I began to think, well, maybe the law could catch up with changes in society, and that was an empowering idea. The notion was that law was, yes, a way to earn a living, but also to do things that would make life a little better for your community.

The number of women who have come forward as a result of the #MeToo movement has been astonishing. My hope is not just that it is here to stay, but that it is as effective for the woman who works as a maid in a hotel as it is for Hollywood stars.

You can disagree without being disagreeable.

My mother was a powerful influence. She made me toe the line. If I didn't have a perfect report card, she showed her disappointment.

When
contemplated
in its
extreme,
almost any
power looks
dangerous.

It's the expectation. You have a lowered expectation when you hear a woman speaking, I think that still goes on. That instinctively when a man speaks, he will be listened to, where people will not expect the woman to say anything of value. But all of the women in my generation have had, time and again, that experience where you say something at a meeting, and nobody makes anything of it. And maybe half an hour later, a man makes the identical point, and people react to it and say, "Good idea." That, I think, is a problem that persists. Some of it is getting over unconscious bias by becoming conscious of it ...

Time is on the side of change.

I think a woman's voice and a woman's experience makes a difference in some cases. I think of the eighth grader who was hauled into the girls' restroom and strip-searched because it was suspected that she had pills— drugs—with her. It turned out to be two Advil. Her mother was incensed that her daughter was so humiliated. So she brought a lawsuit against the school district, and at the oral argument there were jokes about, "Oh, the boys undress in the locker room, nobody thinks anything of it." I just stopped that conversation by saying, "A 13-year-old girl is different than a 13-year-old boy. She's at a vulnerable stage and very self-conscious and embarrassed by showing herself to other people." I think that everybody suddenly realized—yes, they have daughters and there is a difference.

If a judge is called an activist, you know the person saying that doesn't like the decisions.

I'm sure I've changed my mind about something. Inevitably, when we grow up – as we get more experience and wiser. Well, I've changed my mind about some food that I didn't like when I was young.

All I can say is I am sensitive to discrimination on any basis because I have experienced that upset.

This wonderful woman whose statue I have in my chambers, Eleanor Roosevelt, said, "Anger, resentment, envy. These are emotions that just sap your energy. They're not productive and don't get you anyplace, so get over it." As I said before, maintaining a sense of humor is important.

If I had any talent in the world ... I would be a great diva.

The word [feminist]
means that women,
like men, should
have the opportunity
to aspire and achieve
without artificial
barriers holding them
back. It's not that you
don't like men but
that you are for equal
citizenship stature of
both.

If you're going to change things, you have to be with the people who hold the levers.

Sometimes people say unkind or thoughtless things, and when they do, it is best to be a little hard of hearing — to tune out and not snap back in anger or impatience.

The emphasis must be not on the right to abortion but on the right to privacy and reproductive control.

The stain of generations of racial oppression is still visible in our society and the determination to hasten its removal remains vital.

[The right to abortion] is central to a woman's life, to her dignity. It's a decision that she must make for herself. And when government controls that decision for her, she's being treated as less than a fully adult human responsible for her own choices.

We live in an age in which the fundamental principles to which we subscribe —liberty, equality and justice for all — are encountering extraordinary challenges ... But it is also an age in which we can join hands with others who hold to those principles and face similar challenges.

I said on the equality side of it, that it is essential to a woman's equality with man that she be the decision-maker, that her choice be controlling.

The entering class I joined in 1956 included just nine women, up from five in the then second-year class, and only one African American. All professors, in those now-ancient days, were of the same race and sex.

Reacting in anger or annoyance will not advance one's ability to persuade.

It's not simply to say, "My colleagues are wrong and I would do it this way." But the greatest dissents do become court opinions and gradually over time their views become the dominant view. So that's the dissenter's hope: that they are writing not for today but for tomorrow.

I had no role models among women because there really were no women lawyers or judges. Maybe Amelia Earhart, because she was doing something that women didn't do. Otherwise, it was fictional characters such as Nancy Drew.

I really concentrate on what's on my plate at the moment and do the very best I can.

Neither federal nor state government acts compatibly with equal protection when a law or official policy denies to women, simply because they are women, full citizenship stature — equal opportunity to aspire, achieve, participate in and contribute to society based on their individual talents and capacities.

[My husband] Marty was an unusual man. In fact, he was the first boy I knew who cared that I had a brain.

The label "liberal" or "conservative," any – every time I hear that, I think of the great Gilbert and Sullivan song from "Iolanthe." It goes, "Every gal and every boy that's born alive is either a little liberal or else a little conservative." What do those labels mean? It depends on whose ox is being gored.

I don't like to pigeonhole people or give categorical answers. There are some singers that know exactly when to go, and others hang on much too long …

Reading is the key that opens doors to many good things in life. Reading shaped my dreams, and more reading helped me make my dreams come true.

[D]o things in your community — I'm sure you will find things. Whether it's assisting in getting food to the homeless people or if you care about the environment, helping keep local parks clean. And anything that you can do to make things a little better in your community.

We're still striving for that more perfect union. And one of the perfections is for the "we the people" to include an ever enlarged group.

As we
live,
we can
learn.

Women's rights are an essential part of the overall human rights agenda, trained on the equal dignity and ability to live in freedom all people should enjoy.

I think members of the legislature, people who have to run for office, know the connection between money and influence on what laws get passed.

Feminism ... I think the
simplest explanation,
and one that captures
the idea, is a song that
Marlo Thomas sang,
"Free to be You and
Me." Free to be, if you
were a girl—doctor,
lawyer, Indian chief.
Anything you want to
be. And if you're a boy,
and you like teaching,
you like nursing, you
would like to have a

doll, that's OK too. That notion that we should each be free to develop our own talents, whatever they may be, and not be held back by artificial barriers—man made barriers, certainly not heaven sent.

I pray that I may be all that [my mother] would have been had she lived in an age when women could aspire and achieve and daughters are cherished as much as sons.

I have yet to see a death case among the dozen coming to the Supreme Court on eve-of-execution stay applications in which the defendant was well represented at trial... People who are well represented at trial do not get the death penalty.

You can't have
it all, all at
once. Who —
man or woman
— has it all, all
at once?

It is as though a special, zestful spice seasons my work and days. … Each thing I do comes with a heightened appreciation that I am able to do it.

People who have been hard working, tax paying, those people ought to be given an opportunity to be on a track that leads towards citizenship, and if that happened, then they wouldn't be prey to the employers who say, "We want you because we know that you work for a salary we could not lawfully pay anyone else."

Our strategy was the soul of simplicity. It was to go after the stereotypes that were written into law and to show that many could be disadvantaged by the stereotype,

as well as
women. We
wanted people to
be judged by
what they do, by
the functions they
perform, and not
by gender.

[W]hen I'm sometimes asked when will there be enough [women on the supreme court]? And I say "When there are nine." People are shocked. But there'd been nine men, and nobody's ever raised a question about that.

When a thoughtless or unkind word is spoken, best tune out.

The law that the Supreme Court establishes is the law that they must live by, so all things considered, it's better to have it clearer than confusing.

Reproductive choice has to be straightened out. There will never be a woman of means without choice anymore. That just seems to me so obvious. The states that changed their abortion laws before Roe are not going to change back. So we have a policy that only affects poor women, and it can never be otherwise.

I became a
lawyer for selfish
reasons. I thought
I could do a
lawyer's job
better than any
other.

I ... try to teach through my opinions, through my speeches, how wrong it is to judge people on the basis of what they look like, color of their skin, whether they're men or women.

I'm a very strong believer in listening and learning from others.

One thing that I did feel in law school was that if I flubbed, that I would be bringing down my entire sex. That you weren't just failing for yourself, but people would say, "Well, I did expect it of a woman." It's like they would say about a woman driver. So I was determined not to leave that impression.

In the '50s, too many women, even though they were very smart, they tried to make the man feel that he was brainier. It was a sad thing.

Jane was 14 months old when I started law school. There was a break in my day so I worked very hard until 4 o'clock in the afternoon, then I came home and it was Jane's time. So I would play with this little child and then by the time Jane went to bed, earlier than most children, then I was happy to go back to work. Also I realized there was something else in life beside studying hard in law school. I realized that in a devastating way when this little child of mine was creeping along the floor and (suddenly) she has a mouth full of mothballs. I had just put some sweaters away in the drawer. I had to take her to the Cambridge City Hospital to get her stomach pumped. I can remember hearing her screaming. That really brought home to me that there are things in life other than law school. Each part of my life was a respite from the other. Taking care of Jane was fun and reading to her was fun. Two totally different lives that I was living at the time, each one was a respite from the other.

A gender line … helps to keep women not on a pedestal, but in a cage.

The young people that I see are fired up, and they want our country to be what it should be. One of the things that makes me an optimist are the young people.

I've learned … to seek ever more the joys of being alive, because who knows how much longer I will be living?

[When I was faced with the daunting prospect of starting law school with a toddler, my father-in law told me,] "If you really want to study the law, you will find a way. You will do it." I've approached everything since then that way. Do I want this or not? And if I do, I'll do it.

I think we
understand that
for the Court to
work well, we
have to not
only respect
but genuinely
like each other.

The worst times were the years I was alone. The image to the public entering the courtroom was eight men, of a certain size, and then this little woman sitting to the side. That was not a good image for the public to see.

Women will have achieved true equality when men share with them the responsibility of bringing up the next generation.

Promoting active liberty does not mean allowing the majority to run roughshod over minorities. It calls for taking special care that all groups have a chance to fully participate in society and the political process.

I am ever
hopeful that if
the court has a
blind spot
today, its eyes
will be open
tomorrow.

It's a facet of the gay rights movement that people don't think about enough. Why suddenly marriage equality? Because it wasn't until 1981 that the court struck down Louisiana's "head and master rule," that the husband was head and master of the house.

I think our
system is
being
polluted by
money.

On the day I was
married, my
mother in law…
took me aside and
said she wanted
to tell me what
was the secret of
a happy marriage:
"Every now and
then it helps to be

a little deaf." … That advice has stood me in good stead. Not simply in dealing with my marriage, but in dealing with my colleagues.

If you have a caring life partner, you help the other person when that person needs it. I had a life partner who thought my work was as important as his, and I think that made all the difference for me.

I try to teach through my opinions, through my speeches, how wrong it is to judge people on the basis of what they look like, color of their skin, whether they're men or women.

Every constitution written since the end of World War II includes a provision that men and women are citizens of equal stature. Ours does not.

Over my lifespan I think I have had it all. But in different periods of time things were rough. And if you have a caring life partner, you help the other person when that person needs it.

I do think that being the second [female Supreme Court Justice] is wonderful, because it is a sign that being a woman in a place of importance is no longer extraordinary.

I think
daughters
can change
the
perception
of their
fathers.

I grew up in the shadow of World War II. And we came to know more and more what was happening to the Jews in Europe. The sense of being an outsider — of being one of the people who had suffered oppression for no … no sensible reason … it's the sense of being part of a minority. It makes you more empathetic to other people who are not insiders, who are outsiders.

What's the
difference between
a bookkeeper in
New York's
Garment District
and a U.S.
Supreme Court
Justice?

One generation.

q: *How would you like to be remembered?*

[As] someone who used whatever talent she had to do her work to the very best of her ability. And to help repair tears in her society, to make things a little better through the use of whatever ability she has. To do something, as my colleague David Souter would say, outside myself. 'Cause I've gotten much more satisfaction for the things that I've done for which I was not paid.

My mother told me two things constantly. One was to be a lady, and the other was to be independent.

Printed in Great Britain
by Amazon

50851612R00069